Did you know that frogs are cannibals,
fashion can be fatal and the dinosaurs
never died? Or that redheads were
once burned at the stake as witches?
Find out why rubbish tips are like lasagna,
and how maggots help solve crimes!

Books to make
your brain bulge!
find out all about them on
www.itstrue.com.au

HEATHER CATCHPOLE
AND VANESSA WOODS

PICTURES BY HEATH McKENZIE

IT'S TRUE!

SPACE TURNS
YOU INTO
SPAGHETTI

ALLEN&UNWIN

First published in 2006

Copyright © text Heather Catchpole and Vanessa Woods 2006
Copyright © illustrations Heath McKenzie 2006
Series design copyright © Ruth Grüner

Allen & Unwin
83 Alexander Street
Crows Nest NSW 2065
Australia
Phone: (61 2) 8425 0100
Fax: (61 2) 9906 2218
Email: info@allenandunwin.com
Web: www.allenandunwin.com

National Library of Australia
Cataloguing-in-Publication entry:

Catchpole, Heather.
It's true! space turns you into spaghetti.
Includes index.
ISBN 1 74114 625 9.
1. Outer space – Juvenile literature. I. Woods, Vanessa.
II. McKenzie, Heath. III. Title. (Series : It's true! ; 16).
520.

Series, cover and text design by Ruth Grüner
Cover photographs: NASA
Set in 12.5pt Minion by Ruth Grüner
Printed by McPherson's Printing Group

1 3 5 7 9 10 8 6 4 2

**Teaching notes for the It's True! series are available
on the website: www.itstrue.com.au**

CONTENTS

WHY SPACE?

Everyone has questions about space. Could aliens really exist?
How can I become an astronaut? How did the universe begin?
In writing this book, we found the answers to these questions,
and all sorts of other astounding things. Did you know that two-thirds
of the universe is invisible? Do you want to find out how to keep an
ear out for aliens, or what happens if you go too close to a black hole?
Come on a voyage through our Solar System and into outer space.
But be careful – the universe is such a far-out place, you may never
want to come back!

Heather Catchpole

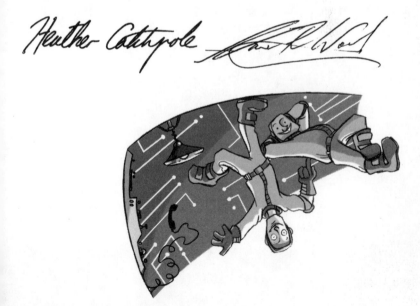

1

SPACE ADVENTURERS

For thousands of years, people have wondered what it would be like to visit space. According to Chinese legend, a Chinese general who wanted to get closer to the stars strapped himself to a chair with 47 rockets! He never made it back, so we don't know what he saw along the way. Since then, many other people – and some animals – have journeyed into space, and from these explorations we've learnt amazing things about our Solar System.

It was just 45 years ago that we first fulfilled our dream of travelling into space. Since the first space flight we have made astounding progress, and may soon walk on our red neighbour Mars. But how did space travel begin, who else has been, and why aren't we on Mars already?

FIRST UP, THE RUSSIANS

The journey into space is fraught with danger. Humans and animals have given their lives so that we can learn more about what lies beyond our planet.

The first human in space was a Russian pilot named Yuri Gagarin. He grew up on a farm near Moscow, and was training to become a metalworker. His teachers said he was hardworking, but a bit of a troublemaker at

IN MEMORY OF
YURI GAGARIN
FIRST MAN IN SPACE, APRIL 12, 1961

FROM THE ASTRONAUTS OF THE UNITED STATES OF AMERICA.

JOHN H. GLENN, Jr.
for
MERCURY ASTRONAUTS

JAMES A. McDIVITT
for
GEMINI ASTRONAUTS

NEIL ARMSTRONG
for
APOLLO ASTRONAUTS

school. He learned to fly light aircraft as a hobby, but this soon became a full-time obsession. He was a daring pilot, and his skills and raw nerve led him to be one of twenty pilots chosen for the Soviet Space Program.

The pilots went through a series of tough physical tests. Yuri passed them all, and was chosen to be the first pilot to leave the Earth.

In the 1950s and 1960s the Americans and the Russians were fiercely competing to launch the first human into space. When Yuri was strapped into his spacecraft, Vostok 1, he knew the Russian people were barracking for him.

Despite the intensive training and simulations he'd been through, no one knew what the effects of space flight would be, or whether Yuri would come back alive. It was thought humans might explode in space, others thought blood would boil.

Yuri said later that as he blasted off on 12 April 1961, he felt as though there was a heavy weight pressing down on him. It was just like the pull backwards you feel when you're in a car that speeds up, but much stronger. As he escaped the Earth's gravity, he became weightless, and objects floated around him.

Yuri's spaceship was so fast that in less than two hours it went around the entire Earth. It returned at 27 000 kilometres (16 777 miles) per hour. Yuri saw flames licking at his window, but special shielding on the outside kept him safe. When he was six kilometres

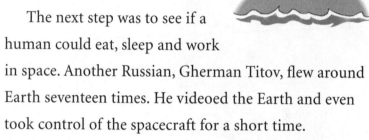

(almost four miles) from Earth, he ejected himself, still in his chair. A parachute opened, carrying Yuri safely to earth, alive and victorious. He had proved that humans could survive in space. In honour of his accomplishment, a crater on the Moon was named after him.

The next step was to see if a human could eat, sleep and work in space. Another Russian, Gherman Titov, flew around Earth seventeen times. He videoed the Earth and even took control of the spacecraft for a short time.

Gherman was the first human to get spacesick – he threw up all his food, and every time he turned his head he felt nauseous. It was a problem space travellers would encounter for decades.

Since our first short trip into space, humans have lived for days, even months, in space. But how long could we survive? Could we even exist on Mars?

BREATHE DEEP

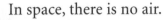

In space, there is no air.
There are gases, but
they are there in
such tiny amounts
that we could never
breathe properly.
To go into space, we
have to carry our own
air. Spaceships and
spacesuits must have
all the right gases,
especially oxygen,
at the right pressure,
and must be absolutely
leakproof.

We also have to control the temperature because
space is extremely cold. If you climb a mountain,
you'll notice the air gets colder the higher you go.
This is because the air is thinner higher up. In space,
where there is no air, it can be freezing.

SUNBURN

Space is only cold in the dark areas.
In the middle of our Solar System is
a ball of furiously burning
gas – our Sun. If your
skin came into
direct contact
with sunlight in
space, you would
be badly burned. Spacecraft are heavily
armoured to protect humans from the Sun's radiation.
Even so, when astronauts are travelling past the Sun
they must be careful not to get caught in a solar flare –
an explosion on the Sun's surface many times more
powerful than an atomic bomb.

FEEL THE FORCE

If you took a trip in a spacecraft, your body would
become lighter as you experienced the weightlessness
of space. If you undid your seatbelt, you'd find you

could walk on the ceiling, turn somersaults in mid-air, and pick up other passengers with your little finger!

The downside is that you might vomit. Astronauts often feel spacesick, because without the Earth's gravity their brain is confused about which way is up or down. Their faces become puffy and their legs look a bit like a chicken's because gravity no longer pulls the blood to their feet. You can experience almost the same feeling if you stand on your head. The blood rushes to your face, and drains from your legs.

A long-lasting effect of zero gravity is muscle weakness. We use all sorts of muscles every day, to lift up our feet, to stand upright, and even to sit on a chair. This is because gravity is constantly pulling downwards, and our muscles have to work against it. In space, we don't need to use our muscles. After a long voyage, astronauts sometimes have to be carried out of their spaceship because they are too weak to walk.

So far, the difficulties of space travel have stopped us venturing far from Earth. Scientists are working to solve them, so we can spend longer in space and see the wonders of the Solar System for ourselves.

ANIMAL ASTRONAUTS

HUMANS AREN'T THE ONLY CREATURES THAT HAVE BEEN INTO SPACE. CHECK OUT WHO ELSE BLASTED OFF AND WHEN.

1946 The first living creatures launched into space were fruit flies that were sent into space with corn seeds. They were sent to test the effect of radiation at high altitudes.

1949 What do you get when you cross a monkey with an astronaut? A monkeynaut! The first monkeynaut was a squirrel monkey called Albert II.

1950 The first mouse in space was sent by the USA. The USA launched several other mice in the next ten years, but the first mouse was the only one to survive.

1957 The first creature to make a complete orbit of Earth was a female dog called Laika, which is Russian for 'barker'.

1961 Just before Yuri Gagarin became the first human in space, a chimpanzee called Ham blasted off. He was trained to pull levers in exchange for rewards. Ham showed that it was possible to perform tasks in space.

1963 Felix the cat went into space.

1968 The first creature sent beyond the Solar System was a Russian tortoise.

1970 Two bullfrogs were launched into space so scientists could better understand space motion sickness. It's the sense of balance in our ears that makes us spacesick, and a frog's ear is very similar to ours.

These are only a few of the creatures that have seen space. Newts, nematodes and even swordfish have been sent into space. Wouldn't it be interesting if they could talk!

2

SO YOU WANT TO BE AN ASTRONAUT?

If you'd like to be an astronaut, you'd better start planning ...

★ Read everything you can about space travel, planets, galaxies, and how we're going to get there.

★ It helps if you speak another language (especially Russian), since you'll be talking to people from all over the world.

★ In high school and university, you'll have to get the best grades you can in subjects like engineering, physics and maths.

★ Also, see if you can get some work experience at your local observatory or radio telescope.

★ Most importantly, you have to be able to get along with people, and work well in a team.

Over 4000 people apply to join NASA's space program every year, and only 100 of these are chosen for the two-year training program. If you're accepted, you'll have to study really hard and pass tests like swimming up and down a pool in sneakers and a spacesuit!

If you do well, you'll be an astronaut after two years. That's when you get into the fun stuff. You'll learn how to launch, orbit and land a spacecraft in preparation for your big journey. Finally, you'll be assigned to your first mission. You could be the first person to land on Mars, float through Neptune or collect ice crystals from Saturn's rings.

SUITS AND SHIPS

Space is a hostile place for Earthlings. Our survival depends on creating an Earth-like environment that we can take with us. Our spaceships and spacesuits must withstand temperature extremes and radiation. They have to provide air pressure to prevent our blood from boiling. It's true! They also have to provide enough oxygen for us to survive the journey.

If you want to buy a spacesuit, you'll have to start saving now – they cost $15 million! They're like mini spacecraft. Spacesuits have to be very tough to protect you from micro-meteoroids – small bits of dust or rock that fly through space. So they are made with lots of layers of tough

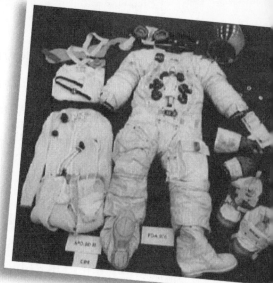

fabrics like dacron or kevlar. You wouldn't want to rip your suit on the surface of the Moon. Spacesuits are also coated with mylar to reflect radiation, and the helmets are designed like tinted polarised sunglasses. It's very bright out there.

Did you know spacecraft enter Earth's atmosphere backwards? The most dangerous part of any mission is returning to Earth. When a spacecraft approaches, it is travelling at 24 times the speed of sound. As it slows down, the energy of its motion turns into massive amounts of heat, enough to melt most metals. To help the craft cope with the heat, it's best to present a blunt object to the hot air, and this blunt object is the spacecraft's behind! Only when the spacecraft has completely slowed down does it turn around. However, everything is still very hot, so the front part of a spacecraft is lined with heat-resistant metal called a heat shield.

Scientists are constantly working on films, composites, adhesives, coatings, paints, and parts that will make space equipment stronger and safer. They're inventing things like huge solar sails that can harness enough solar energy to power the spacecraft, and metal that repairs itself when it is hit by an asteroid. And for missions to Mars, they're even thinking of using the astronauts' wee and poo

to protect the spacecraft from radiation! Waste from the toilet and maybe garbage will be hardened and patched on to the outside of the spacecraft which will stop the radiation from burning the metal. Let's hope the smell doesn't get in!

SPACE TOURISM

If you want to go to space but don't like the thought of all that maths, there might be a way for you to visit without any study at all! Space tourism is about to take off. In 2001, American businessman Dennis Tito was the world's first tourist to leave Earth. He flew on a Russian spacecraft and stayed a week at the International Space Station. His ticket cost a whopping $20 million.

Now, the race is on to make space a holiday destination. On 4 October 2004, SpaceShipOne became the first re-usable aircraft designed especially to take tourists to space. And that's not all. Space Island Group plans to build a space city 600 kilometres above the Earth, out of empty NASA space shuttle fuel tanks.

WHAT IF THINGS GO WRONG?

You need to be very brave to be an astronaut.
No matter how much protection you have, or how
carefully the journey is planned, things can still go
wrong. There are millions of individual parts on a
spacecraft, and just one tiny malfunction can lead to
tragedy. Humans have been journeying into space for
over 40 years. We've come a long way, but in that time
we've had some disasters, and some very near misses!

SPACE DISASTERS

Apollo 13 was the most famous near-disaster in the
history of space travel. The year was 1970. During the
flight to the Moon, there was a loud bang, the ship
shuddered and power supplies dropped. The crew
didn't know what had happened, but they quickly
discovered that both their oxygen tanks had been
damaged. The oxygen was used to create electrical
power for the craft so they were in serious trouble.
The crew of Apollo 13 abandoned their planned

Moon landing and started the journey back to Earth. But there was only enough power in the back-up battery for 10 hours and they were 87 hours from home.

By the time they approached Earth, they were running out of oxygen. Their cabin was a chilly three degrees Celsius because they couldn't waste precious energy on heating. But the worst was yet to come. With limited power, they couldn't rely on their instruments to guide them back to Earth. This was a big problem as the angle of re-entry had to be precise and the spacecraft was still surrounded by smoke from the explosion so they couldn't navigate by the stars either. Too shallow, and they would skim off the Earth's atmosphere and bounce back into space. Too deep, and they would explode into a fireball.

OXYGEN LEVELS

TOO MUCH
GROOVY
RELAX
OKAY
HMM...
UM...
UH OH!
OH NO!!!
WHAT OXYGEN?

People around the world were glued to their TVs, and held their breath as Apollo 13 prepared for re-entry. Thousands cheered wildly as the luckiest astronauts on the planet made it safely home. Afterwards, NASA investigated the incident and discovered that exposed electrical wiring had ignited an oxygen tank, causing an explosion. They modified the craft to make sure it would never happen again.

Your parents will remember the day the Challenger exploded. On board was Sharon McAuliffe. She was to be the first teacher to visit space, and schoolchildren were watching the launch live on TV, in classrooms all over the USA.

It was the coldest launch in history, with the temperature a near-freezing 2 degrees Celsius

(36 degrees Farenheit). Less than one second after blast-off, black smoke started to pour from Challenger's right rocket. The smoke turned into flame, which came into contact with thousands of litres of explosive hydrogen in the fuel tank. Just 73 seconds into its journey, the Challenger exploded, killing all seven crew members. NASA staff later found out that the extreme cold had damaged a rubber seal, called an O ring, in the right rocket. Gas had leaked out from the damaged seal and caught fire, causing the explosion.

The Columbia accident was recent enough for you to remember. It was 1 February 2003. The spacecraft launched perfectly, and no one knew anything was wrong until re-entry. Columbia was travelling at 18 times the speed of sound, when it exploded, killing all seven people on board. In Texas, people heard a loud bang and saw a bright light and smoke plumes. Hours later, pieces from the spacecraft fell to earth.

An investigation committee was set up to find the cause of the Colombia explosion. It discovered that during take-off a piece of foam on the outside of the fuel tank had broken off and smashed into the wing, damaging the heat-protection tiles. This wasn't a problem until the shuttle re-entered Earth's atmosphere, and the wing over-heated. It looks as though freezing conditions at the time of the launch caused the malfunction in the first place.

Even though missions into space can be so dangerous, most astronauts make it safely home. The more we practise, the better we get at space travel. Maybe one day you'll jump on a shuttle to Mars as casually as you'd hop on a bus to school.

3

ROCKY WORLDS

Would you like to live on another planet? Before you decide, let's take a quick look at our own Earth, the perfect home for humans, animals and all other known forms of life.

There are several reasons for choosing to live on Earth. The most important is that Earth has an atmosphere which allows us to breathe. There's plenty of oxygen, and there are other gases that reflect sunlight back to Earth, keeping us warm and comfortable.

There's also plenty of water in the oceans that helps to even out the climate. Earth has another special feature: the rocks that make up the Earth's crust are constantly being sucked into the Earth's hot, melted interior and spat out again from volcanoes. This process, called plate tectonics, has played a big role in shaping our planet. It's the ultimate source of our atmosphere and may have played a role in creating the conditions necessary for life.

FIRST STOP: THE MOON

If you were heading into space, chances are you'd stop off first at the Moon. The Moon is the only object in space that humans have walked on. In the future, it could be a good place to refuel before going on a long journey to the other planets.

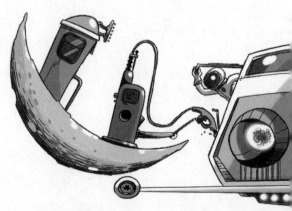

The Moon has no atmosphere, and its surface is covered by craters left by falling meteorites. (Meteors also fall to Earth but most burn up before they

reach us.) The biggest impact crater on the Moon is Tycho. You can easily see Tycho using a good pair of binoculars or a telescope.

Have you ever wondered why you always see a face or the 'Man in the Moon'? The Moon rotates around us every 29½ days and it takes roughly the same time to rotate on its own axis. Because of this, we only ever see one face of the Moon. We call the other side of the Moon the 'lunar farside'. Until the 1960s, when the Soviet Union photographed it, and the Apollo 8 to 17 spacecraft mapped this side of the Moon, no one had seen this landscape.

VENUS AND MERCURY – BEHIND THE SUN

Venus is the closest planet
to Earth, orbiting between
us and the Sun. Although it
is similar in size to Earth,
Venus is a very different
place. If you stood on the
surface you would be choked
by its hot, poisonous
atmosphere and drenched
in acid rain.

Unmanned spacecraft
have descended through Venus's thick atmosphere
and mapped its flat lands and few towering mountains.
They discovered two raised areas of land or 'continents',
called Ishtar and Aphrodite. The continents contain
volcanoes, deep rift valleys and mountainous land that
proves Venus's crust is still moving.

Mercury is a tiny world of extremes. If you landed
on Mercury, you would be hot as an oven or freezing,

depending whether or not you were on the side facing the Sun. From day to night, the temperature drops over 500 degrees Celsius (932 degrees Farenheit)!

Because it is closest to the Sun, Mercury orbits faster than the other planets, so its year is very short. It speeds around the Sun every 88 days. Because it rotates on its axis very slowly, one day on Mercury is 59 Earth days. Mercury rotates differently to all the other planets. Because its day is so long and its year is so short, a funny thing happens when the Sun rises. Shortly after sunrise the Sun sets and then rises again. You actually see a sunrise happen twice in one day!

MARS – THE RED PLANET

If humans do land on another planet, it is most likely to be one of the closest and most well-known of our neighbours, Mars.

Mars is red because of the rusted iron in its sand and rocks, just like the deserts in central Australia. We know a lot about the rocks of Mars because they have been photographed by spacecraft orbiting the planet. There are currently two Mars rovers, called Spirit and Opportunity, exploring the craters and wide plains.

The Mars rovers have discovered evidence that the planet was once drenched in water, which has since evaporated. Some water remains frozen under the surface and in thick icecaps at the poles. If these icecaps melted, maybe Mars would start to transform into a planet we could live on.

Gravity is greater on Mars than on the Moon because Mars is bigger, about half the size of Earth. You wouldn't need a bulky spacesuit to walk on the surface.

But you would still need a helmet – Mars has a very thin atmosphere and there is very little oxygen for you to breathe.

Some of the awesome features you can see on Mars are the Valles Marineris, a canyon which is bigger than any on Earth, and Olympus Mons, the tallest volcano in the Solar System.

Mars also has two small moons called Phobos and Deimos (meaning 'fear' and 'panic'). They are probably asteroids that were caught in the planet's gravity, unlike our Moon which was formed from the debris left over when something huge, like another planet, collided with the Earth.

ROBOTS IN THE SKY

Five, four, three, two one . . . Blast Off!

Humans have never been further than the Moon, so robotic spacecraft are our only way to gather information and take pictures of the Solar System. These spacecraft have travelled to the Moon, visited Neptune and Uranus, and photographed the surface of Mars. Future spacecraft missions are set to visit most of the planets in the Solar System.

Missions planned for the future include the Prometheus Jupiter Icy Moons Orbiter (JIMO) spacecraft, due to be launched in 2011. JIMO will explore Jupiter's three planet-sized moons, Callisto, Ganymede and Europa, to look for evidence of water.

The Rosetta spacecraft will try to land on a comet in 2014. It will fling an anchor on to the comet, then touch down using its 'icepick' legs. This will help astronomers understand more about how these so-called 'dirty snowballs' form.

In two million years, one of the first spacecraft to leave our Solar System, Pioneer 10, will reach another star. Pioneer 10, launched in 1972, was in 1973 the first spacecraft to visit Jupiter. By the time it reaches the star Aldebaran in the constellation of Taurus, humans may have left the confines of our Solar System and travelled past Pioneer 10 on their way to explore the rest of the universe. Next stop, outer space!

THE ASTEROID BELT

Between Mars and the outer planets is the asteroid belt. This rocky ring holds cratered rocks of all shapes and sizes. Some are shaped like commas, and one looks like an enormous dumbbell. Scientists think the asteroids are the shattered remains of rocky bodies that smashed together as the planets formed. It would take three days to drive around the largest asteroid, Ceres.

The asteroid belt is the source of most meteoroids. Rocky bodies wobble out of their orbit and shoot through space towards the inner planets and their moons. Many meteoroids have hit Earth in the past, and scientists think that one such impact may have wiped out the dinosaurs.

Once you zoomed through the asteroids in a spaceship, the spectacular sight of the giant gas planets would greet you. Jupiter and Saturn are huge balls of gas surrounded by rings and moons.

HEAVENS ABOVE!

ALL THE PLANETS APART FROM EARTH
ARE NAMED AFTER ROMAN GODS.

Speedy **Mercury** is the gods' messenger.

Venus is the goddess of love.

Mars is the god of war.

Giant **Jupiter** is the leader
of the gods.

Saturn is the god of the harvest.

Uranus is the father of Jupiter
and the earliest supreme god.

Neptune is the god of the sea.

Pluto is the god of the
underworld, the Roman
version of hell.

4

THE GAS GIANTS

KING OF THE PLANETS

Jupiter is the biggest of all the planets. Guess how many Earths would fit inside Jupiter – 1300!

All we can see of Jupiter are the clouds on its surface. The famous 'red spot' is a storm that has been raging since humans first focused telescopes on it 300 years ago. Winds howl around Jupiter in hurricanes so big they are called hypercanes. Lightning crashes through its atmosphere of hydrogen and helium.

Jupiter protects the inner planets of the Solar System from collision by pulling asteroids towards itself with its massive gravity. The gravity is so strong that one of its 63 known moons, Io, is stretched out of shape. This stretching heats the moon, making it the most volcanically active body in the Solar System.

Jupiter's four biggest moons are clearly visible from Earth through a small telescope and were discovered long before the others by the scientist Galileo in 1610. They are called the Galilean moons. You can see them through a good pair of binoculars.

The largest moon, Ganymede, is the size of a small planet. Like Io, Ganymede is rocky and has mountains and valleys. Jupiter's second largest moon, icy Callisto, has a surface battered by meteorites. Europa, the next largest, is covered in cracked ice. Scientists think that this could be because there is liquid underneath, maybe even water.

Future missions will explore these moons to find out if they contain liquid water, and if some form of life is present.

You'll find out more about space missions (and alien-hunting) in the next few chapters. But right now our next stop in the Solar System is the most spectacular planet of them all.

SATURN – LORD OF THE RINGS

Saturn is one of the most beautiful sights in the Solar System. Jupiter, Uranus and Neptune also have thin rings, but Saturn's glittering, banded rings are unique. They are only a few hundred million years old, much younger than Saturn itself. Scientists think the rings may have formed as a passing comet broke up, or a moon was shattered by a collision.

Saturn's rings are divided into seven smaller rings labelled from A to G, but because some of them were discovered later they are not named in order. The outermost ring is 420 000 kilometres (260 976 miles) from the cloud tops of Saturn.

The rings are made of particles of ice and rock ranging in size from the microscopic to large boulders. Some are pink and others are grey and brown. Different-coloured rocks within the ice cause the different colours.

Saturn is mostly hydrogen and helium, with some ice, and frozen ammonia and methane. There are no rocks on the surface. If you landed on Saturn, you would sink into the clouds.

You couldn't live on Saturn, but you might be able to live on Saturn's largest moon, Titan. Half Earth-size, Titan has a surface that is a mixture of ice and hydrocarbons – the molecules necessary for life. The spacecraft Cassini and the probe Huygens (a smaller spacecraft that was dropped down to Titan) have revealed that the surface has river channels and probably has lakes of liquid methane.

URANUS AND NEPTUNE – ICE SISTERS

Once your spacecraft reaches Saturn you are more than 1.4 billion* kilometres (870 million miles) from the Sun. Travel the same distance again and you reach cold blue Uranus. A gas giant with an inner rocky core, Uranus has a temperature of about minus 214 degrees Celsius (417 degrees Farenheit). It is tilted on its side, possibly because of an enormous collision, and rolls around its orbit like a ball rather than spinning like a top, as the other planets do. Its nine dark rings and 27 moons may have formed at the same time as the collision.

If you travel 2 billion kilometres further still you'll encounter Uranus's sister planet Neptune,

* That's 1400 000 000!

which is similar in size, colour, temperature and composition. Neptune has fewer rings and moons (four rings and 13 moons) but rages with storms as big as Jupiter's and has the fastest winds in the Solar System. The winds blow at 2100 kilometres (1305 miles) per hour – that's about eight times as fast as a cyclone!

PLUTO – END OF THE LINE

Last and smallest of the planets, Pluto is the final stop in the Solar System. You are now almost 6 billion kilometres (3.7 billion miles) from the Sun.

Earth	6,000,000,000
Neptune	Much closer
Charo	Right next door

Icy Pluto has a satellite called Charon (*kar*-on). Charon rotates around Pluto but is half Pluto's size, so it is sometimes called a twin planet rather than a moon. While Pluto is made of rock and ice, Charon is mostly made of ice, and has a thin, scanty atmosphere. Pluto's atmosphere freezes, then vaporises again, as it moves away from and then closer to the Sun.

SPACE TELESCOPES

Everything we know about the outer reaches of our Solar System and beyond comes from telescopes and robot spacecraft that allow us to explore space without leaving our own back yard.

The biggest telescope in space is the Hubble Space Telescope (Hubble for short), which orbits 600 kilometres (373 miles) above Earth. Its main mirror is only 2.4 metres (2.6 yards) across, but because it is in space where the light from the stars is not affected by the Earth's atmosphere, Hubble can help us see more clearly into the Universe than larger land-based telescopes. The telescope has to be very steady, and accurate. For Hubble, locking on to distant stars and planets is the equivalent of you focusing a beam of light on a 5-cent coin more than 300 kilometres (186 miles) away.

Hubble gave us the first evidence of a black hole several billion times heavier than the Sun, and has since proven that black holes are found at the centre of nearly every galaxy. With its help we have seen 12 billion light years into space, to the very edges of the known universe.

A new telescope is now being built that will pick up infra-red light – light we can't see with the naked eye. Called the James Webb Space Telescope, its 6.5-metre (7.1 yard) mirror will dwarf Hubble. It is scheduled to launch in 2011. Scientists hope it will help reveal the shape of the Universe, explain the birth of galaxies and stars, and explore mysterious dark matter.

COMETS

Pluto and Charon are part of another belt of icy debris that orbits the Sun, called the Kuiper Belt. This is one source of comets, dirty balls of ice that speed around the Sun in long orbits. Immediately beyond the Solar System, astronomers think there is a cloud of ice and gas, called the Oort Cloud. Passing objects jolt hunks of icy matter out of this region in space, sending them hurtling into orbit around the Sun as comets.

As comets approach the Sun, their ice melts, combines with dust and spreads out behind them in a glowing tail. Many comets pass Earth regularly. We see them as star-like objects with fuzzy tails. In the past, people thought comets were omens and blamed them for their troubles and misfortunes.

HOW FAR OUT
IS THE SOLAR SYSTEM?

Start with a new roll of toilet paper,
a marking pen, and a long corridor.

Beginning at the end of the toilet roll, mark the
Sun on the very edge of the first sheet. A little
more than one-third of a sheet away from the Sun,
put a small 'm' for Mercury. Three-quarters of a sheet
away from the Sun, put a 'V' for Venus.

At the start of the second sheet, put an 'E' for Earth.
This length, one toilet sheet, represents about
149 597 871 kilometres (92 955 807 miles), which is
the average distance between the Earth and the Sun,
called one solar distance or 1 AU (Astronomical Unit).

Halfway along the same sheet, mark a big 'M' for Mars.
Jupiter is a little more than five sheets and Saturn is
nine-and-a-half sheets out from the Sun.

Roll the toilet paper out to mark the distant planets
Uranus (19 sheets), Neptune (30 sheets)
and Pluto (39 sheets).

Remember that planets can be closer to or further
from the Sun, depending what point of their orbit
they are in. The distances between planets and
the Sun change because their orbits are
not exactly circular.

5

TO INFINITY
AND BEYOND

Outside our Solar System, the vast cold depths
of space extend further than we can imagine.
The distances are so great that even light, which
reaches us from the Sun in just over eight minutes,
takes millions and even billions of years to arrive
from the far reaches of the Universe.

Get the picture? Space is B-I-I-G. But it's not
as empty as it seems. As we gaze into the dark
spaces, we are discovering the mysteries of the
stars. How do they die? How many are in a galaxy?
And much, much more!

TWINKLE, TWINKLE LITTLE STAR

Stars twinkle because of the way their light passes through the Earth's atmosphere. They may look like diamonds in the sky, but stars are actually fiery balls of gas undergoing powerful nuclear reactions to create light. Most stars burn hydrogen and helium. Our Sun does the same – and without this source of energy, life could not exist on Earth.

There are many different kinds of stars. We sort them into categories based on their size, colour, brightness and stage of development.

Our Sun is yellow because it is a medium-hot star. The outer layer of the Sun's atmosphere, called the corona, is about 2 million degrees Celsius (1.8 million degrees Farenheit). The Sun is hottest at its core where the temperature is about 15 million degrees Celsius (27 million degrees Farenheit).

The hottest stars are blue-white and are seven times hotter than the Sun. Red giants, such as Antares in Scorpius, are the least hot stars, even though they are the largest.

STARGAZING

Different cultures see different pictures in the stars. What looks like a fish to some might be a peacock to others. When you look up at the night sky, keep an eye out for a lion, a bear, a dragon, a scorpion, a flying horse, a queen, a prince, and a hunter standing on a magic river. Our ancestors imagined stars were the realms of gods, and gave many of the stars and constellations their own story.

The Incas thought that each one of their tribes originated from a different constellation. Every part of their lives was written in the stars. They believed the Milky Way was a sacred river that linked the living world to the dead.

Ancient civilisations placed great importance on astronomical events, such as the summer and winter solstices. They made detailed calendars and built temples and pyramids that lined up with the stars, Sun and planets. Stars were the guiding light for sailors at sea, and caravans in the desert. Newborn babies were given detailed star charts that foretold their future.

Chinese astronomers have been keeping detailed records of the stars and planets for a very long time. They used the records to determine the seasons and the passage of time. In 1054, Chinese astronomers witnessed a supernova in the area of the sky we now call the Crab Nebula. They called it a 'guest star'. It was so bright, it was visible during the day. The Chinese were also the first to record a solar eclipse, in 2136 BCE.

Ancient Greek astronomers used mathematics to understand stars and our place in the Universe. Most of them thought that the Earth was the centre of the Universe. Earth was seen as the planet chosen by the gods – the Sun and everything else revolved around us. A Greek scholar, Aristarchus (310–230 BCE), was the first person we know who said that the Earth might orbit the Sun. But until Copernicus (1473–1543 CE), most people continued to believe that the Earth was at the centre of the Solar System.

IT'S TRUE! THE SUN WILL EXPLODE

Stars do not burn for ever. As they grow old, they expand. When they have burned all their hydrogen and helium fuel, the core begins to contract and the outer layer cools and dims. Eventually the core collapses. What happens next depends on the size of the star.

Stars the size of our Sun last about 10 billion years. Somewhere in the Milky Way, a star like our Sun dies approximately once every month. In 2003, the Hubble telescope brought us images that showed us what the death of our Sun might look like. In the next few billion years, the Sun will start to run out of fuel. The core of the Sun will shrink and become incredibly hot, inflating the outer layers until it becomes a bloated red giant that will engulf Mercury, Venus and Earth.

When all the hydrogen and helium fuel is used up, the core of the Sun will contract further still, and its atmosphere will drift off into space like smoke rings. All that will be left is a core of carbon and oxygen. This core will cool down and collapse to form a small white dwarf star, not much bigger than Earth.

The white dwarf doesn't burn like a star any more, but is surrounded by glowing gas called a planetary nebula. Eventually the glow will be extinguished and our Sun will be left as a cold ball of carbon called a black dwarf.

GIANT STARS

When a giant star dies, its core starts to shrink, until the star is only a few kilometres across. The core heats to billions of degrees and finally explodes in a massive supernova – one of the most violent explosions in the Universe.

All that is left of the star after that is a ball of tiny particles called a neutron star. Neutrons are part of what is inside atoms, the building blocks that make up everything, from stars to our bodies.

A neutron star is tiny but very dense and heavy. In a space the size of a football field, it packs in about the same mass as 25 million African elephants! Some neutron stars send out beams of light and are called pulsars. They pulse so accurately they are known as the clocks of the Universe.

GALAXIES

Our Sun is one of millions of stars on the outer edge of our galaxy, the Milky Way. When you look up at the thick band of stars that sweeps across the night sky, you are seeing the stars at the centre of the galaxy.

Galaxies are made up of billions of stars, planets and other inter-stellar matter like gas and dust. They come in different shapes and sizes. Our Milky Way is a spiral galaxy. Others look like footballs, clouds or discs.

Next to the Milky Way is the Canis Major dwarf galaxy. Our other neighbours, which you can see on very dark nights in the Southern Hemisphere, are the Magellanic Clouds. These cloud-shaped galaxies are much smaller than ours.

Our nearest large galaxy neighbour is another spiral galaxy, Andromeda. Because it is so far away, Andromeda looks like a faint, smudged star to the naked eye.

CLUSTERS AND SUPERCLUSTERS

Scientists classify galaxies in giant groups called clusters. The Milky Way, Andromeda and a few smaller ones make up the Local Group. The next closest group is the Virgo Cluster. It is much bigger and contains

thousands of galaxies. It's so big it would take light 10 million years to travel from one side of the cluster to the other.

A collection of clusters is called a supercluster. The Virgo Cluster is at the centre of the Virgo Supercluster, which is is 100 million light years across.

It's so big that the light we are seeing now, from the other edge of the Virgo Supercluster, was made in the days of the dinosaurs!

Our local supercluster is shaped like an oval pancake.

THE INVISIBLE UNIVERSE

Between the clusters and the super-clusters are huge stretches of space. But they aren't totally empty. When scientists recently calculated the mass of all the Universe they could see, they found that the stars, planets and galaxies didn't account for all the mass. There was something else out there. Something that weighed about 30 trillion trillion trillion trillion tonnes, about 73 per cent of the mass of the Universe. Scientists called it 'dark matter'.

Dark matter is invisible. No one knows what it is made of, how it got here or why there is so much of it. Astronomers will be working hard to solve the mystery of dark matter with new telescopes and space missions.

THE EDGE OF THE UNIVERSE

At the very edges of the Galaxy are powerful objects called quasars.

The most distant quasars are so far away that it takes their light 13 billion years to reach us. They shine brighter than 100 galaxies combined. The light we see from some quasars was created when the Universe was very young. Studying quasars can help us learn more about the beginning of the Universe.

Recently, we have been able to see planets in orbit around some very distant stars. But who lives there? Are there aliens in our Galaxy, or even in our own Solar System? And if there are, can we call them up to ask them over for pizza?

6
ALIEN-HUNTING

Have you ever looked up at the stars and wondered if anyone lived out there? Maybe, somewhere on another planet, an alien is looking at Earth and asking the same question.

We have wondered about aliens for thousands of years. What would they be like if we found them? Would they be friendly, or would they come with sinister plans to destroy Earth? No one knows if aliens exist, but that hasn't stopped us looking.

WHERE WOULD THEY LIVE?

Astronomers generally agree that stars are too hot for aliens to live on. Aliens are much more likely to be found on a planet similar to Earth that orbits a star like our Sun. In 1961, a scientist called Frank Drake developed a formula to guess how many of these planets might exist in the Universe.

The formula looks like this:

$$N = R^* \cdot f p \cdot n e \cdot f l \cdot f i \cdot f c \cdot L$$

The equation looks complicated, but it's just a series of questions. How many stars are in the Milky Way? How many stars have planets around them? How many planets have life? And could that life communicate with us?

At the moment, the Drake equation predicts that there are 1000 planets in the Universe that could be home to aliens who are able to communicate with us. If there are planets out there with aliens, how do we find them?

Since humans haven't been around for very long compared to the Universe, our technology is not very advanced. Our main hope is that aliens have been around for much longer, and have developed more advanced technology. Maybe they have already started looking for us! Most of our alien-hunting involves searching for signals. If the aliens are out there, maybe they are trying to get our attention.

LIGHT

If aliens were trying to get our attention, one way would be to flash a light at us, just as you would flash a torch if you wanted someone to find you in the dark. Some scientists think that aliens might shine a laser beam because lasers are powerful enough to reach different planets.

We have several telescopes that scan the sky for brief pulses of light that might be alien lasers. One telescope in Harvard, Massachusetts has a special camera with over a thousand detectors that can spot flashes of light as brief as a billionth of a second.

The problem with sending light messages is that aliens would have to send the messages directly to Earth, which means they would have to know exactly where we were. Our telescopes have picked up many strange light signals, but most of them are created by starlight or other normal things in the Universe. However, as technology improves, we could develop a telescope that is able to ignore these false alarms, and find out if there are any aliens shining their torch at us in the dark.

RADIO

Radio waves are easier
signals for us to find.
Radio waves travel at the same
speed as light. If aliens are sending them,
they don't have to know exactly where we
are, they can just send the radio waves into
space, and we can detect them.

To detect radio signals, we use a radio telescope
that is similar to the radio that you have in your house
or your car (only bigger). There are two ways you can
search for radio signals. The first way is to look at
large chunks of the sky (about a million stars worth),
one at a time. If a signal is detected, you can zoom the
telescope in for a closer look. The second way is to
zoom in closely
from the start
and investigate
1000 stars at
a time.

However, like the light signals, there are a lot of false alarms. The Universe is a noisy place, and the radio waves that telescopes detect could be made by anything from colliding asteroids to exploding stars.

RECORDS

Another way we could contact aliens is to send them gift-wrapped packages of information. The Voyager Golden Record is a 30-centimetre (12-inch) gold-plated copper disc that carries sounds of life on Earth. There is a copy of the record travelling on board the robotic space probes Voyager 1 and 2, which are headed out of our solar system on their journey to distant stars. Some of the sounds on the record are natural, like wind, thunder and rain, and some are made by people. There is music, including Chuck Berry's *Johnny B Goode* (your parents will know that one), Mozart's *Queen of the Night Aria* from 'The Magic Flute', and a song by African pygmies. There are also greetings from Earthlings in 55 languages, as well as a personal message from Jimmy Carter, who was the president of the USA in 1977, the year the Voyager spacecraft were launched.

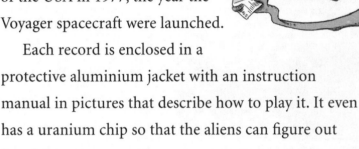

Each record is enclosed in a protective aluminium jacket with an instruction manual in pictures that describe how to play it. It even has a uranium chip so that the aliens can figure out how long ago we sent it.

Voyager 1 sped past Pluto in 1990, and left our Solar System in 2003. It's expected to reach the nearest star in 40 000 years. Perhaps one day an alien will walk into his back yard and find a strange package has crashed into his garden. Maybe he will open it up and see a shining gold disc and its picture instruction manual, all ready to go.

Though it has never been proven, some people are convinced that aliens have visited Earth already.

There have been thousands of sightings of Unidentified Flying Objects (UFOs), but almost 90 per cent were discovered to be natural or human-made phenomena like aircraft, satellites, blimps, balloons, clouds, the northern lights, fireworks, meteors or ball lightning. However, a few of the sightings could not be explained. If they were alien spacecraft, we will probably never know, since proof is almost impossible to find. But this doesn't stop people believing. The study of UFOs is called – you guessed it – ufology.

Crop circles are large patterns that appear in grain fields. The patterns are usually circles, which has led some people to think they were made by landing spacecraft. Since the 1970s, thousands of crop circles have appeared all over the world, from Russia to England, America and Japan. At least some of them were pranks. Ten years after the first crop circles appeared, two men stepped forward to claim that they had been making them using planks, rope, hats and wire.

LOOKING FOR ALIENS

Would you like to help search for aliens? You don't need a telescope. You don't even need binoculars. All you need is a home computer and the Internet.

One of the problems when looking for aliens is that once a telescope has captured information from space, it takes a long time and a lot of energy to process it. A group of astronomers called SETI (Search for Extraterrestrial Intelligence) have found a way to connect millions of home computers, so they can untangle the information collected by a telescope.

FIND AN ALIEN

The first step is to download a program from the Internet called SETI@home.

Go to http://setiathome.ssl.berkeley.edu

A radio telescope in Puerto Rico collects information from space and sends small amounts of information to your computer. When you aren't using your computer, a screensaver comes on that decodes the information from the telescope. When your computer has finished, it sends the information to a university in America where astronomers check if your computer has found anything.

Home computers have already found strange signals from outer space, and astronomers are trying to work out what they are. It could be your computer that picks up an alien's message!

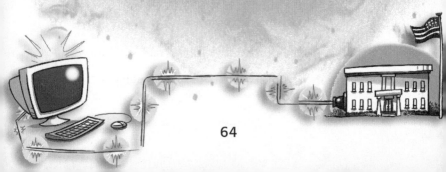

FLYING SAUCERS

The name 'flying saucer' came from American businessman Kenneth Arnold in 1947. He claimed he saw nine UFOs hurtling by at incredible speed way up in the air. He said they looked like saucers skipping over water, and the name has been used ever since.

ALIENS ON MARS

So far, we have not found any little green people on Mars, but that does not mean there's no life at all.

Scientists have found small amounts of a gas called methane in the Martian atmosphere. Methane is not a stable gas, and quickly breaks down into water and carbon dioxide. This means something on Mars is continuously making methane. On Earth, living creatures make methane. You produce it when you burp or fart. Methane is made by volcanoes. It is also made by tiny living organisms called methanogens, which don't need oxygen to survive.

If Mars has these tiny creatures, it would mean that it is not a dead planet. If a planet close to us has life, then we can guess that many other planets in the Universe have life on them as well.

Even though these Martians would be more like bacteria than little green people, discovering life on Mars would change the way we saw the Universe for ever.

DRAW AN ALIEN

What special adaptive features would they have?

★ Large eyes to see in the dark?

★ Large ears to hear radio waves?

★ Blue skin to blend in with their atmosphere?

★ A heavy body or a light body to suit
the gravity of their planet?

★ Strange noses or mouths to breathe
in a different atmosphere?

★ Fins, flippers or tails if they lived
in the ocean?

★ What else?

7

BLACK HOLES REALLY SUCK YOU IN

Ever heard of a black hole? No, it's not the hole in your stomach where all your food disappears. It's a hole in space from which nothing, not even light, can escape! It's true, the Universe is full of holes – and some of them are so big, they could swallow an entire solar system.

WHAT IS A BLACK HOLE?

A black hole is an object whose gravity is so strong that not even light can escape. It's made when matter is squished up very tightly. Black holes are so dense that they could fit our whole Sun into an area the size of a pinhead!

There are big black holes, and REALLY big black holes. The smaller ones are called stellar black holes, and they can vary from just a few times the mass of our Sun (called a solar mass), to 100 times the mass of the Sun (or 100 solar masses). REALLY big black holes are called supermassive black holes. They are more than a million times the mass of our Sun!

HOW TO MAKE A BLACK HOLE

Stellar black holes (the smaller ones) are found in lots of galaxies, including the Milky Way.

They are created when giant stars explode in a supernova. After the explosion, all that is left is a neutron star. It's tiny compared with the original star but it's very dense.

If the giant star that made it was big enough, the neutron star continues to collapse. It becomes so small and dense, and its gravity is so strong, that eventually it becomes a black hole.

WHY ARE BLACK HOLES BLACK?

If you throw a rock into the air, it will fall back down, because the gravity of the Earth is pulling it back. The harder you throw it, the longer it takes to drop back to Earth.

If you had superhuman strength, and could throw the rock so far that it travelled beyond the Earth's gravitational force, it would float into space. The speed at which you would have to throw an object to escape gravity is called escape velocity. The escape velocity of Earth is 11.2 kilometres (7 miles) per second. If you could throw a rock so that it travelled 11.2 kilometres per second, it would escape Earth's gravity and drift into space.

Black holes have an escape velocity that is faster than the speed of light (299 792 kilometres, or 186 282 miles, per second). Since nothing can travel faster than light, it means everything that comes close to a black hole is sucked in. Nothing can escape, not even light.

HOW TO FIND A BLACK HOLE

No one can see a black hole because there is nothing to see. They're invisible! So how do we know they are really there?

Famous physicist Albert Einstein talked about black holes long before people found any evidence for them. We can now prove that black holes exist by the effect they have on other things in space. Stars and gases orbiting a black hole are sped up by its gravity. So astronomers look for stars and gas moving faster than they normally would.

When a black hole swallows something, it sends out a big burp in the form of a flash of X-rays. Astronomers look for these X-rays for more evidence that a black hole is really there.

REALLY BIG BLACK HOLES

Scientists think that super-massive black holes exist at the centre of most galaxies, including a monster one at the centre of our own Milky Way which is almost three million times the mass of the Sun! No one knows how these giants form, but there are many different theories. They might begin life as stellar black holes which grow and grow as they swallow the stars and gas that cluster at the centre of every galaxy. Black holes grow in proportion to the material they suck in – the more they swallow, the bigger they get. Another theory is that several stellar black holes get mashed together, forming a giant black hole.

Recently astronomers have discovered middle-sized black holes in star clusters away from the centre of the Milky Way. Finding out more about these could help astronomers learn more about gravity, and how giant black holes form.

WATCH OUT!

Imagine you are cruising through the Universe in your spaceship. All of a sudden, you feel like you are going faster than you are supposed to. You look ahead – there are no stars or planets to pull you in by their gravity, but

you are speeding up all the time.
Soon, you lose control. There is
nothing ahead except for an
uncomfortable darkness, void of stars.
Then something really weird starts to
happen. Your feet stretch out in front of
you, as if someone were pulling on them.
Your whole body begins to stretch out long
and thin like a piece of spaghetti. Too late, you
realise you have been sucked into a black hole.

WHAT HAPPENED?

On the edge of a black hole is an invisible
barrier called the event horizon.
Beyond the event horizon, nothing can
escape. It's the point of no return.

If you crossed the event horizon in
your spaceship, you would be crushed by
the enormous gravity. Although it would
be over very quickly, it could produce
some strange effects. If your feet were

closest to the centre of the black hole they would be sucked in first. Your body would stretch out in a process called 'spaghettification'.

Even time is warped by the gravity of a black hole. Many science-fiction TV shows, books and movies have suggested that entering a black hole could send you into another dimension, or an alternative universe where everything is different. Maybe you could even travel through time. But whether you turn into spaghetti or become a fearless explorer of strange universes, there's no doubt that black holes are fascinating places!

8

THE BEGINNING OF THE UNIVERSE

How did this amazing Universe, full of strange galaxies, black holes, exploding stars and crashing meteorites, all begin?

Our Universe, as we know it, began about 14 billion years ago. Before then, nothing existed. No stars, no planets, and no people. At the very beginning of time, the Universe was concentrated in a tiny point, smaller than you can see and hotter than you can imagine.

the UNIVERSE
- life size

Then, for reasons which no one completely understands, the Universe suddenly popped into existence. This moment of creation is called the Big Bang.

The Universe expanded to become large enough to hold all the planets, stars and galaxies. But it didn't stop there – it kept getting bigger and bigger (and still is!).

I S'POSE THAT'S PRETTY BIG - I GUESS!

Lots of scientists came up with the Big Bang theory, but it wasn't proven until Edwin Hubble (the same Hubble who had the telescope named after him) came along in 1929. Hubble noticed that all the galaxies were moving away from us. He also saw that the further away the galaxies were, the faster they were going. This proved that the Universe was still growing.

More evidence for the theory came from the discovery of the radiation left over from the Big Bang. Cosmic Microwave Background Radiation is similar to the microwaves you use at home to cook food. We now know that Cosmic Microwave Background Radiation comes from all over space. When we use special telescopes to collect these microwaves, we can see that the brightness of the radiation is the same in all directions on the sky. The only explanation for this is that the Cosmic Microwave Background Radiation was present at the very beginning of the Universe and spread as the Universe expanded.

THE EARLY UNIVERSE

Just after the Big Bang, there were no stars or galaxies. The Universe was extremely hot – millions of times hotter than lava from a volcano. As the Universe cooled, tiny particles formed which later combined to form the atoms that are part of all of us. These particles are the building blocks for everything, from galaxies to stars to planets. They even make up the

blood, skin, hair and fingernails that are part of you!

Eventually, giant balls of particles formed. They were made of hydrogen and helium and were several hundred times bigger than our own Sun. This was the first lot, or generation, of stars. Deep inside their cores, the early stars created heavier elements like oxygen and carbon. The stars burned fiercely and brightly but, because they used up so much fuel, they could not burn for very long. After only a few million years, they exploded. The violence of the explosions scattered the heavier particles throughout the Universe, and these formed a new generation of stars.

THE BALLOON UNIVERSE

MATERIALS

★ Balloon ★ Coloured markers

To understand how the universe expands, imagine you are sandwiched in the skin of a balloon. You live IN that surface and, for you, there is no up or down. Draw a dot, which represents you. Then, draw coloured shapes on the balloon to represent the galaxies.

Blow up the balloon in one long, slow breath. As the balloon inflates, you will see all the galaxies around your dot move away. As the balloon gets bigger, the galaxies will move away from your dot faster and faster.

This is the way the universe is expanding, with everything moving away from everything else.

LONELY STARS

The second generation of stars were made of carbon and oxygen, but not much iron. They lived longer than the first stars, but had a lonely existence. They had no planets like the Earth orbiting them, because they didn't have enough heavy elements to form the solid bodies of rock from which the Earth was formed. (Earth, for example, has lots of iron, silica and magnesium.) But when these stars exploded, heavier elements were created, which would eventually form solid planets like our Earth.

So the whole process repeated itself again, and a third generation of stars was born, stars more like our Sun. As they formed, a swirling disc of gas and dust collected around them. This gas and dust was either pulled together by gravity, or collided with other gas and dust in the disc to form bigger and bigger bits called planetoids. Eventually our Sun, and the planets of our Solar System, were born.

If the Universe began with a bang, how will it end? Some think it might rip, others think it might

freeze. No one really knows, but it's something we don't need to worry about for billions of years. The Sun will keep burning for at least another 5 billion years. By that time, humans might be living on other planets, near other stars, or even in other galaxies. Perhaps we will be travelling through time, and communicating with intelligent life from other solar systems. Maybe we will be shooting through black holes and coming out in entirely different universes – anything is possible!

So now you know some of the things we've learned about space in the 45 years since Yuri Gagarin strapped himself in and blasted off. It's exciting stuff.

But exploring space isn't just about adventure. It makes us appreciate what a beautiful planet we live on. The blue haze of our precious atmosphere, the abundance of the ocean, and the green continents all combine to make a safe haven in this corner of the galaxy, a haven we call home.

As astronomers probe the darkest, furthest corners of our Universe, new theories are created, old ones are tossed aside, and arguments are begun that last lifetimes. But however the Universe began, and however it will end, one thing is certain: the answers we're finding are astonishing, intriguing and so incredible that we'll never stop exploring space.

HEATHER CATCHPOLE has been interested in space ever since she saw Halley's Comet. Her biggest space thrill was seeing a bolide (a large meteor) burn up in the atmosphere. She writes regularly for kids and adults in science books, magazines and online.

Heather is an ABC broadband TV and web producer and the author of four science books and a book of poetry.

VANESSA WOODS started making her own constellations in the sky when she was about five. She found a dragon, a poodle and a bunyip right next to the Southern Cross.

Her most interesting jobs have been chasing monkeys in Costa Rica, and filming in Antarctica where she made friends with a penguin called Bob.

Vanessa is now a writer and lives in Germany.

HEATH McKENZIE has illustrated more books and magazines than he can count on two hands – he blames toys, cartoons and old movie posters for the way his drawings look. Oh, and he's a big fan of robots and spaceships . . . and monkeys (preferably combined)!

THANKS

Thanks to John Storey, Tony Trouvillon and John Webb from the University of New South Wales; Scott Croom from the Anglo Australian Observatory; Malcolm Walter from the Centre for Astrobiology and Darren Osborne from CSIRO.

Thanks also to Cody Horgan and Ted Catchpole for their continuing inspiration and to Bronnie: one day you'll go to space and beyond.

Heather Catchpole and Vanessa Woods

The publishers would like to thank istockphoto.com and the following photographers for photographs used in the text: page 56 Michael Knight and page 64 George Cairns. Thanks to NASA for all other photographs used in the text. Thanks also to Fred Watson, Astronomer-in-Charge at the Anglo-Australian Observatory in Coonabarabran, for checking the text.

WHAT TO LOOK OUT FOR

★ **Sirius**, the brightest star in the sky.

★ **Venus**, called the morning and evening star because it is the brightest star in the sky at dawn and dusk.

★ The **Southern Cross**, one of the most recognisable constellations, looks like a cross with an extra star.

★ (In summer) **Orion**, the hunter.

★ (In winter) **Scorpius**, the scorpion.

IN DARK SKIES

★ The bright band of the **Milky Way**.

★ The **Coal Sack**, a dark patch of sky beside the Southern Cross.

★ The **Magellanic Clouds**, irregular galaxies that appear as fuzzy patches near the Milky Way.

WHERE TO FIND OUT MORE

Websites

- http://www.abc.net.au/science/space

The ABC space home page, this site contains lots of regularly updated news and information about all things space.

- http://www.nasa.gov/audience/forkids/home

The NASA website for kids has lots of information, including regular updates about current missions.

- http://spacekids.hq.nasa.gov

A NASA website devoted to space science for kids.

- http://science.howstuffworks.com/space-channel.htm

Explanations about how and why all sorts of space stuff works.

- http://hubblesite.org

Information on the Hubble telescope and general astronomy, including beautiful photos taken by Hubble.

- http://marsrovers.nasa.gov/home/index.html

This website lets you follow the day-to-day progress of the Mars rovers, Spirit and Opportunity.

- http://earthobservatory.nasa.gov

Beautiful and interesting images of Earth from the NASA satellite network.

For teachers

- http://www.nasa.gov/audience/foreducators/5-8/features/index.html

NASA's website for educators includes learning resources, NASA contacts and useful web links.

- http://www.museum.vic.gov.au/planetarium/index.html

The home page of the Melbourne Planetarium at Scienceworks

- http://www.csiro.au/index.asp?type=educationIndex

The education website of the CSIRO regularly features space science.

INDEX